PLANT-BASED 🌿 POINT
BEEFLESS CAKES
EASY PLANT-BASED RECIPES featuring BEEFLESS CAKES

food photography & recipes by

Robin Coarts

Jules Schnedeker

with portrait and quote contributions from our beautiful "beefless cakes"

BEEFLESS CAKES:
Easy Plant-Based Recipes featuring Beefless Cakes

Published by:
Plant-Based Point
70 SW Century Dr
Ste 100 PMB 5001
Bend, OR 97702

ISBN: 978-1-7370650-0-5
Library of Congress Control Number: 2021907912

This book is intended for informational and entertainment purposes only and is not intended to be used as or construed as medical advice. Please consult a healthcare professional regarding any nutritional or allergen guidance.

Design + photography
by
Robin Coarts + Jules Schnedeker
with portrait + quote contributions by our "Beefless Cakes" + Michelle Fetsch

1st Edition, 2021

For more information, please visit: https://plantbasedpoint.com.

To all of those who've felt the nudge to create a better world,
one beefless cake at a time

Contents

From Our Kitchen to Yours

What's up, you fine piece of grass?! Thanks for grabbing hold of our beefless cakes; we promise it'll be a feast for the eyes and the stomach.

By purchasing this cookbook, you've supported an independent, women-owned business AND made a donation to a worthy cause - a portion of the proceeds from this book will be given to badass vegan organizations and changemakers.

In this book, you'll find some of our favorite easy, affordable, plant-based recipes alongside vivacious vegans sharing their plant-based points (why they're vegan). These beautiful beefless cakes all live their best lives without any help from animal products. We hope these stories and recipes inspire you in the kitchen and beyond!

Share With Us

We love seeing your kitchen handiwork. Tag @plantbasedpoint
across social media to share your creations!

You can also find recipe videos and cooking tutorials on our YouTube channel (@plantbasedpoint). Happy ogling, er, cooking!

Sincerely,

robin +
jules

proud founders of
PLANT-BASED 🌿 POINT

Notes

Disclaimer: We rarely measure! Not because we're experts, but because we gravitate towards very forgiving recipes. We hope this gives you the confidence to experiment and have fun in the kitchen - make our recipes your own!

Throughout this cookbook, we'll refer back to this section, because almost all of our recipes can withstand ample substitutions and swaps while still remaining delicious. Gluten-free? Oil-free? Soy-free? Nut-free? We got you!

Making potato salad and hate raw red onion? Leave it out! Or hey, add some Caramelized Onions (page 52). Whoa. We never thought of that before. See? Go nuts! Unless you have a nut allergy. Then please see the following page.

Furthermore, you can alter many of our seasoning suggestions, or even omit altogether, without compromising the end result.

don't have fresh herbs?
no problemo!

Substitutions + Swaps

Oil or vegan butter	Water or vegetable broth (with the exception of spanakopita, mushroom gravy, and wine sauce. For baked goods, you can use applesauce)
Nuts	Many nuts are interchangeable or can be substituted with shelled sunflower seeds or pepitas
Soy	Where we use tofu as protein, you can easily swap for beans or plant-based meat. For tofu ricotta, you can use boiled cauliflower. For ranch dressing, you can use soaked, raw cashews
Gluten	Feel free to use gluten-free flours, pie crusts, breadcrumbs, and pastry, etc.
Onions	Skip or substitute with celery or shallots where appropriate
Fresh vs. dried herbs	Generally 1 teaspoon dried = 1 tablespoon fresh

Equipment

Many of our recipes utilize a food processor or blender. If you're doing a lot of plant-based cooking, we highly recommend investing in a food processor and high-powered blender - especially for blending nuts. If you don't have a high-powered blender, you can soak your nuts overnight or simmer for 20-30 minutes before blending.

In some cases, using a hand mixer or finely chopping ingredients will work. Not sure you'll make good use of a new kitchen appliance? Don't be shy about begging, borrowing, or stealing (just kidding), or check online for refurbished items to help both your wallet and the planet.

Lastly, most of our recipes don't require special pots or pans in specific sizes, meaning you can use almost any size frying pan, large saucepan, or pot. Robin loves to use her cast iron skillet for nearly all of her savory recipes and recommends lowering the heat just slightly if you're doing the same.

Other Notes

STORAGE

We didn't include storage instructions for each recipe as they all follow the same general rule: Store refrigerated, in an airtight container, for up to 5-7 days. We have noted which recipes freeze especially well on the individual recipe pages.

SERVING SIZES

Many of our recipes can be used as appetizers or mains, dips or spreads, so depending on how you choose to serve them, the yield will change. We've included serving sizes in each recipe, but you'll often find a range for this reason. In general, all of our recipes serve between 4-8.

VARIETIES

We often say "any variety onion" or "any kind of oil" and don't suggest specific brands for vegan dairy/meats. This is because our recipes are very adaptable to whatever you have on hand/your favorites!

 = serving size one... no?

" I realized eating animal products limited my athletic potential. Once I shifted to a vegan lifestyle, my eyes opened further and I saw that the impact my food choices made environmentally and ethically far exceeded the personal health benefits I've experienced."

Dakota Gale
TraipsingAbout.com

Plant-Based Primer

New to plant-based cooking? Here's a little starter kit to get you going, and you can find even more tips and tools on our website, including a free, printable, plant-based primer: PlantBasedPoint.com.

On the 'Resources' page of our website, we include a lot of our favorite products and brands. With all of the new plant-based items consistently hitting the shelves, this is an ever-evolving list! Here are a few things that never change:

Our pantry must-haves

- Agave
- Coconut aminos
- Coconut milk
- Dried beans (especially chickpeas, mung beans, black beans)
- Grains (brown rice, quinoa, bulger)
- Nutritional yeast (gives your dishes a salty, cheesy 'funk' that you'll grow to love if you don't already)
- Raw cashews
- Spices (especially smoked paprika, garlic powder, dill, oregano)
- Tahini
- Unsweetened plant-based milk
- Vegetable broth

LET'S TALK ABOUT A PRESSING ISSUE

a few tips

PRESSING TOFU

You don't need any fancy equipment! Here's how we do it: (1) Open tofu package and drain excess water. (2) Slice horizontally into three even-sized 'cutlets.' (3) Weave dish towels between each slice and place tofu/towel stack between two plates (make sure the towel is covering each outer edge of your stack). (4) Rest something heavy on the top plate, creating a 'press.' (5) Wait 20+ minutes.

If you purchase vacuum sealed, high protein tofu, you can skip the pressing step and simply squeeze out the excess water by wrapping one dish towel around it and squeezing over the sink. Note: these high-protein tofu packages generally contain more tofu, so if you use them in place of water-packed, firm or extra firm tofu (sold in 12-14 ounce plastic containers), you may want to leave some out or adjust other ingredient ratios in your recipe accordingly.

If you freeze tofu ahead of time and thaw before using, it will press more quickly and yield a chewier texture.

I'm very imPRESSive

a few tips (continued)

BREADCRUMBS

Many store-bought breadcrumbs contain milk, so be sure to check the ingredients label. (Panko breadcrumbs are generally accidentally vegan.) It's also very easy to make your own breadcrumbs. To yield about ½ cup breadcrumbs, dry out or toast two slices of your favorite bread, put them in a food processor, and pulse until they turn to crumbs. (If the bread is dry enough, you can crumble by hand.)

SAUTÉING

Most of our savory recipes start with a cooked onion. Cooking onions in water, broth, oil, or vegan butter until they're translucent usually takes about 5-10 minutes. Don't rush this step or you'll wind up with crunchy onions and less flavor.

Our top go-to's when we just can't even

- Overnight Oats (page 40)
- Pasta with Pumpkin Cream Sauce (page 68)
- Quesadillas or wraps with black beans and Cashew Spread (page 55)
- Soup (most soups are very freezer-friendly!) (page 82)
- Nachos with Cheez Sauce (page 59), black beans, and sliced scallions
- Garlicky Pasta - assembles & cooks in one pot! (page 113)

JULES'S TOP TIP

ROBIN'S TOP TIP

When trying any new plant-based recipes, food items, or products, think of it like switching from an old favorite brand to a new one, e.g., Heinz to Hunts ketchup. The flavor (and maybe texture) might seem REALLY different - because your tastebuds just aren't used to it. **Yet**. But that doesn't mean it's bad! I hated cashew "cheese" (page 55) at first. Now? I can't live without it.

Read recipes before you begin, mark off your likes/dislikes, and dive in. If you don't like onions, skip 'em! If you love beans, double 'em! Don't be afraid to adjust recipes to your preferences. While you're learning recipes, figure out which kitchen tools you *must* have and which ones you can do without. Create a space that works for you and what you're cooking up.

Beefless Cakes

Beany Taco Meat 23

Crabless Cakes 24

Lentil Sloppy Joes 26

Sweet 'n Savory "Beef" 31

Veggie Burgers/
Meatless Balls 33

"Being vegan saved my life! I lost 80 pounds, ditched 12 medications and found a new passion for living. I became a plant-based chef and founded a plant-based food production company, The Kula Connection, LLC all because of plants' amazing power to heal."

Michelle Russell
The Kula Connection, LLC

Beany Taco Meat

serves 4

1 15.5-ounce can (about 1 ¼ cups) kidney beans, drained and rinsed
1 heaping cup walnuts or almonds (see notes)
Fresh cilantro to taste (optional)

SPICES (see notes):

1 teaspoon garlic powder
½ teaspoon onion powder
½ teaspoon paprika
½ teaspoon chili powder
Salt and pepper to taste
-OR-
2 teaspoons taco seasoning

OPTIONAL SPICES (see notes):

½ teaspoon cumin
½ teaspoon coriander
¼ teaspoon cayenne powder
½ teaspoon oregano

Add nuts to food processor and pulse until roughly chopped. Add beans and seasonings and pulse until blended - do not purée. Your mixture should still have a slight crunch.

Serve inside tacos, burritos, or wherever you would normally use seasoned "beef"!

NOTES: You want a ratio of slightly more nuts to beans so your final mixture isn't pasty. The seasoning measurements here are conservative; you may like more!

Play around with seasonings and bean/nut varieties! Want to try "sausage"? Grab white beans and season with fennel seeds, sage, liquid smoke, etc. You can add a splash of soy sauce, vegan Worcestershire, coconut aminos, mustard, vinegar, lemon juice, fresh herbs... you get the idea!

Crabless Cakes

makes 8 cakes

2 14-ounce cans artichoke hearts packed in water, drained and chopped (squeeze out any extra moisture)
¼ cup scallions, sliced
¼ cup red bell pepper, finely diced
¼ cup corn (thawed if frozen)
¼ cup red onion, finely diced
1 teaspoon Old Bay seasoning (see notes)
½ teaspoon salt
½ teaspoon black pepper
¾ cup vegan mayonnaise (see description)
½ cup panko or plain bread crumbs (see notes)

Preheat oven to 350 degrees F. In a large bowl, combine all ingredients. You want enough mayonnaise to bind everything together, but not so much that your mixture becomes goopy. (If you accidentally add too much, toss in more breadcrumbs!) Form mixture into patties (makes about 8), and place on a lightly oiled baking sheet. Bake for 20 minutes, then carefully flip, and bake an additional 20 minutes.

Serve on a salad, as a sandwich, on their own, or with a dipping sauce!

NOTES: To make your own Old Bay seasoning for this recipe, combine: ½ tsp celery salt (or ½ tsp celery seed + ¼ tsp salt), ½ tsp paprika, a pinch of crushed red pepper or cayenne pepper, and a few turns of black pepper.

Check out our 'Tips' section if you want to make your own breadcrumbs, too!

You can also pan fry these. If they fall apart, you may not have added enough mayonnaise or cut your veggies too large. Don't fret! You should be able to press them back together, and once they cool down, they're much easier to handle. You can make these a day ahead and reheat in the oven for a wonderful party appetizer.

Lentil Sloppy Joes

serves 4-6

¼ cup water for sautéing
½ yellow or white onion, chopped
2 cloves garlic, minced
1 red bell pepper, diced
1 teaspoon chili powder
1 teaspoon smoked paprika
3 cups cooked red, green, or brown lentils (see notes)
1 14-ounce can crushed tomatoes (can use fire roasted)
4 tablespoons tomato paste
1 tablespoon maple syrup
½ tablespoon apple cider vinegar
Salt and pepper to taste
¼ cup vegetable broth (optional)

Warm ¼ cup of water in a large saucepan pan over medium heat. Add onions and garlic and sauté for 1-2 minutes. Add red bell pepper and spices, and sauté for another 4-5 minutes. Add tomatoes, tomato paste, and lentils, stir, and turn heat to medium high. Add remaining ingredients (including vegetable broth, if using), stir to combine, return heat to low, and simmer for about 15 minutes. Taste and adjust seasonings as desired.

Serve as is, or with your favorite rolls!

NOTES: Red lentils are our favorite lentil for this recipe and you can use canned lentils. To cook your own lentils yielding 3 cups for this recipe: Simmer 1 ¼ cups lentils with 4 cups water for 20 minutes or until softened. Drain any excess water.

The optional vegetable broth is suggested if your final mixture is sticking to your pan and needs (or you prefer) additional "sloppiness."

> " My mindfulness practice has taught me compassion for all beings. Through enhanced awareness, attention and clarity, I can make more conscientious and humane choices. Being vegan is my recognition that all beings are deserving of life."
>
> Taylor Wagner

> "I'm vegan because the animal agriculture industry is awful for animals, slaughterhouse workers, and our planet. I don't want to contribute to that suffering. Personally, I feel healthier and have become a stronger athlete while eating this way!"
>
> Kelsey Joseph

Sweet 'n Savory "Beef"

serves 4

1 onion (any variety), chopped
2 tablespoons oil (any kind)
1 package (about 12 ounces) of your favorite beefless ground meat
2 tablespoons fresh ginger, minced
2 tablespoons fresh garlic, minced
1/4 cup soy sauce or tamari
3 tablespoons brown sugar
fresh scallions and cilantro (optional, but highly recommended!)

In a large pan over medium high heat, sauté onion in oil until the onion is translucent (5+ minutes). Add beefless crumbles and stir for 2-3 minutes. Next, add garlic and ginger, stirring frequently for another 2-3 minutes. (It will smell amazing!) Then, add soy sauce and brown sugar, stirring until well combined and sugar dissolves. Lastly, top with fresh scallions and cilantro and dig in!

We love this alongside steamed or roasted broccoli, and/or rice. (You can even use it as an alternative filling to our spanakopita pie recipe [page 124])!

Cheez Sauce recipe on page 59!

Veggie Burgers/Meatless Balls

yields 6 medium patties or 12 small meatless balls

½ medium zucchini, shredded
1 cup brown or green lentils, cooked
1 cup oat flour
¼ cup BBQ sauce
⅛ cup liquid aminos
1 teaspoon smoked paprika
1 teaspoon garlic powder
¼ cup water for sautéing
1 onion (any variety), diced
1-2 cloves garlic, minced
¾ cup bread crumbs (see notes)
1 tablespoon nutritional yeast
Salt and pepper to taste

Preheat oven to 350 degrees F. In a medium-sized bowl combine: shredded zucchini, oat flour, liquid ingredients, and spices (not including nutritional yeast). In a large saucepan over medium high heat, warm ¼ cup water. Add onion and garlic and sauté until soft. Next, add cooked lentils, onion, and garlic to blender or food processor and lightly blend - do not over blend, just enough so that ingredients are combined; you still want a noticeable texture.

Mix in ~¾ cup bread crumbs (enough to bind ingredients until they're no longer goopy). Shape into patties and sprinkle nutritional yeast on top. Place on a baking sheet with silicone cover or parchment paper. Bake for 15 minutes, flip over, and bake for an additional 15-20 minutes.

If you want to turn these into meatless balls, simply swap the garlic powder and smoked paprika for oregano and basil! Roll into 12 small balls and bake for the same amount of time (15 minutes, flip over, and bake for an additional 15-20 minutes). Enjoy on a sub or with your favorite pasta.

NOTES: See our 'Plant-Based Primer' section for details on making your own breadcrumbs!

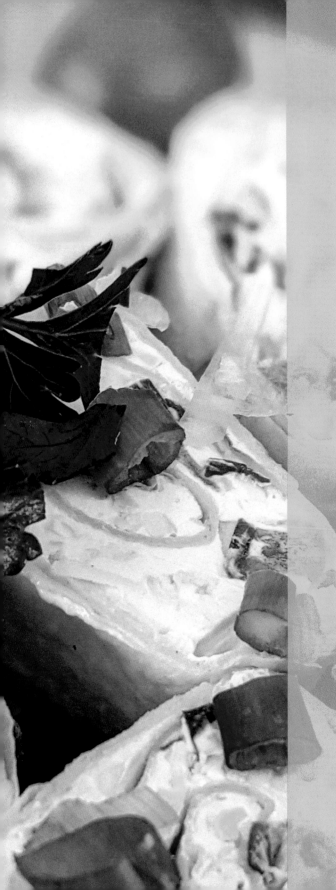

Appetizers + Snacks

Muhammara

serves 6-8

¾ cup bread crumbs (see notes)
1 12-ounce jar roasted red bell peppers (see notes)
1 cup walnuts
1 clove garlic, peeled
Juice from ½ lemon
3-4 tablespoons fresh parsley
4 tablespoons olive oil (you can skip if you're oil-free)
2 tablespoons pomegranate syrup (can substitute with agave or maple syrup)
1 teaspoon dried Aleppo pepper (can substitute with crushed red pepper flakes)
1 teaspoon cumin
1 teaspoon paprika
¼ teaspoon cayenne pepper (optional)
salt and pepper to taste
extra parsley and pomegranate syrup to garnish (optional)

Pulse together all ingredients in a food processor until blended. If you like it chunkier, toss in a few more walnuts at the end and give it a few quick pulses. (Or feel free to use a mortar and pestle to blend!)

Serve with your favorite pita bread, naan, crackers, and/or veggies, or use as a sandwich or wrap spread!

NOTES: Play around with ratios and make sure you give it a day in the fridge before making your final assessment! The flavors really come together after a day.

For ¾ cup bread crumbs, use store-bought or make your own: 3 small slices of bread (we like sprouted), dried out or toasted, then pulsed in your food processor.

Aleppo pepper and pomegranate syrup are usually available at specialty spice shops (or online); they give the most authentic flavor, but we've made this dip using agave and crushed red pepper and it's still delicious!

Mushroom-Walnut Pâté

serves 6-8

½ cup vegan butter or olive oil (or a mixture of both)
1 white or yellow onion, chopped
1 shallot, minced
16 ounces baby bella mushrooms, diced
2-3 cloves garlic, minced
⅓-½ cup fresh parsley, roughly chopped
¼ cup fresh basil -OR- 2 tablespoons fresh sage -OR- 1 tablespoon fresh thyme, roughly chopped
1 cup walnuts
1 tablespoon white miso (optional)
1 tablespoon fresh lemon juice (optional)
⅓ cup dry white wine or champagne to deglaze pan (optional)
Salt and pepper to taste

In a large saucepan over medium high heat, warm vegan butter/oil. Add onion and cook until translucent (5+ minutes). Add mushrooms and continue cooking until mushrooms are completely cooked (15-20 minutes). You can put a lid on your pan to help speed up the process. If mixture begins to stick to bottom of pan, add a splash of water, broth, oil, or wine, and stir. Next, add garlic, herbs, and salt and pepper (and lemon juice and miso paste, if using), cooking for 1-2 additional minutes and stirring frequently.

Turn off heat and set aside. To your food processor, add walnuts and give a few quick pulses. Carefully add your mushroom mixture and pulse until blended, but not pureed.

Serve at any temperature with crackers or crusty bread. For a portable, crowd-pleasing appetizer, consider using this dip as a filling inside phyllo cups (can be purchased frozen as cups, and usually accidentally vegan!).

NOTES: If you don't have a food processor, you can chop your mushrooms and walnuts more finely and mix together in your stovetop pan; the final result may not gel together, but will still taste wonderful and pair well with bread, crackers, etc.

" I'm plant-strong for a billion reasons... for my health, the environment, and for the billions of animals that end up on a plate each year. I eat plant-strong to help create a more compassionate world."

David R. Smith
DSmithFineArt.com

Overnight Oats

serves 2-3

1 cup rolled oats
1 cup non-dairy milk
¼ cup almond butter
1 teaspoon cinnamon
¼ cup sliced strawberries or your favorite berries (can use frozen)
1 tablespoon pecans, chopped
¼ teaspoon chia seeds
Pinch of salt and vanilla (optional)

Combine all ingredients in a medium-sized container and stir. Put lid on and place in fridge overnight. Can be warmed up in the morning if you prefer!

NOTES: Maple syrup, other nuts, and nut or seed butter swirled through make wonderful additions.

" I am vegan because respecting and showing compassion to all life forms is a part of who I am."

Adar Kalter

Plant-Based Pepperoni

yields about 26 1-inch pepperonis

1 package (14-16 ounces) extra firm or firm tofu, pressed
3 ounces tomato paste
1 teaspoon liquid smoke
Olive oil or cooking spray (optional)

Spice mix:
1 teaspoon salt
1 teaspoon black pepper
1 teaspoon red pepper flakes (optional)
2 teaspoons ground mustard
1 teaspoon fennel seeds
2 teaspoons smoked paprika
2 teaspoons garlic powder
2 teaspoons sugar (can substitute brown sugar, agave, or maple syrup)

small water bottle = pepperoni cutter!

Preheat oven to 400 degrees F. Mix the spices and sugar together, then blend everything (except oil) in a food processor until smooth. Dump mixture onto a cookie sheet lined with parchment paper and put another sheet of parchment paper over top. Roll out until it's about 1/4-inch thick (or to your preference). Remove the top piece of parchment paper, spray or coat the top of your pepperoni sheet with oil (optional), and bake for 20 minutes.

Take out of oven, and using a small round cutter (e.g., cordial or shot glass - or small water bottle!), make all of the cuts as close together as possible (as if you were making sugar cookies), leaving everything in place. Bake an additional 10-15 minutes.

Let cool, then carefully remove pepperonis and use to top your pizza(s), saving the extra crumbled parts in an airtight container. (Or do like we do and eat them all while the pizza is in the oven.) You can freeze any leftovers, too!

NOTES: To press tofu, see our 'Plant-Based Primer' section. These aren't your pizzeria style, greasy pepperoni. These are fluffier and less chewy, and utterly addictive. They carry all of the pepperoni flavor with none of the saturated fat or cholesterol.

"I am grateful to have transitioned to veganism and learn that I can thrive on a plant-based diet. The plant kingdom has the nourishment we need and I love demonstrating that through my lifestyle!"

Annika Lundkvist
PedestrianSpace.org
PacificRootsMagazine.com

Spinach Artichoke Dip

serves 6-8

2-3 tablespoons olive oil
1 onion (any variety), chopped
1 14-ounce can artichoke hearts packed in water, drained (squeeze out any excess water) and chopped
12 ounces baby spinach, roughly chopped
3-4 cloves garlic, minced
2 tablespoons fresh lemon juice
1 tablespoon white miso paste (optional)
2-3 tablespoons nutritional yeast
½ cup vegan mayonnaise (can adjust to taste - see notes)
Dash of crushed red pepper, white pepper, and nutmeg (optional)
Salt and pepper to taste

In a large saucepan over medium high heat, heat oil. Add onion and cook until translucent (5+ minutes). Add artichokes, miso paste, and garlic, and stir for a minute. Next, add spinach, lemon juice, nutritional yeast, and seasonings. Continue stirring until spinach cooks down. (Should only take a minute or two.) Turn off heat and stir in mayonnaise.

Serve hot or cold with your favorite crackers, veggies, bread, in a wrap, or even on top of pasta! (We've often made this into farfalle pasta salad with pine nuts and it's a huge hit.)

NOTES: Pureed white beans + plant-based milk, tahini, or vegan sour cream also work in place of mayonnaise. The taste changes with each, but the artichokes and garlic remain your primary flavors!

Tortilla Roll-Ups

Great make-ahead dish!

yields about 20 bite-sized roll-ups

8 ounces vegan cream cheese, softened (see description)
8 ounces vegan sour cream
6-8 ounces vegan cheddar, pepperjack, or colby jack shreds
1/2 cup scallions, sliced
1/3 red bell pepper, finely chopped
4-5 large (burrito-size) tortillas

To soften the cream cheese, rest on counter for a few hours or put in microwave for about 30 seconds. In a large mixing bowl, combine all ingredients and spread evenly on tortillas. Roll up each tortilla tightly and then place in a large, lidded dish (or on a plate, then wrap with foil).

Refrigerate for at least 4 hours (or overnight). Remove from fridge and, using a very sharp, non-serrated knife, slice each tortilla into about 5 bite-sized pieces (not counting the end pieces, which you can snarf while no one's looking).

This is a great make-ahead dish and one of our most popular party appetizers!

NOTES: You can make this oil-free by using oil-free tortillas and filling with refried beans, hummus, or our Cashew Spread recipe (page 55) instead of vegan dairy. Other great fillings include beans, tomatoes, corn, cilantro, jalapeño, and soy chorizo.

Dressings, Spreads + Sauces

Balsamic Marinade/Dressing 50

Caramelized Onions 52

Cashew Spread 55

Champagne Sauce 56

Cheez Sauce 59

General Tso's Sauce 63

Mushroom Gravy 65

Balsamic Marinade/Dressing

serves 6-10+

½ cup olive oil
⅓ cup balsamic vinegar
3-4 cloves garlic, minced
⅓ cup fresh basil, chopped
⅓ cup fresh parsley, chopped
Salt and pepper to taste
Squeeze of fresh lemon juice (optional)
Vegan mayonnaise to taste (see instructions)

One of our favorite plant-based wins: Because you don't have to worry about contamination, you can repurpose any of your marinades for salad dressing!

In a large bowl, combine all ingredients except vegan mayonnaise. Use this mixture to marinate your favorite vegetables or plant-based protein before baking or grilling.

Save any leftover marinade and combine with vegan mayonnaise to make a spectacular dressing packed with flavor. Use your creamy dressing over your cooked/grilled veggies, a salad, as a dipping sauce, or sandwich spread!

" I went from vegetarian to vegan because my 7-year-old daughter did. She knew eating animal products was wrong and I could no longer use the "but cheese is so good" excuse. Now the whole family has been vegan for over five years - for the animals, for the planet, and for our health."

Felicia Greenfield
Board member at
LittleBearSanctuary.org

Caramelized Onions

serves 6-8

4-5 Vidalia onions, peeled, quartered, and evenly sliced
2-3+ tablespoons oil, any kind
2-3+ cups water and/or broth
Salt to taste

In a large saucepan over medium high heat, heat oil. Add your onions and keep an eye on them. Once they start to stick to the bottom of the pan, add more liquid (about ¼ cup) and give them a stir.

Repeat this process every few minutes (once they start sticking to the bottom of the pan) for about 40-60 minutes, and eventually your onions will have cooked down to a beautiful, caramel color and be ready to go! You can add a little salt and bam! Use them in ANYTHING: sandwiches, burgers, nachos, quesadillas, pasta/potato salads, dips, cheese and crackers, etc.! We love pairing it with our Tofu Ricotta (page 76)!

NOTES: This is time consuming, but incredibly simple (and affordable!), and will take your BBQ or weekly meals to the next level. If you're going to be in or near the kitchen prepping other food, this is a fun recipe to toss into the mix now and then. You can speed up the process by turning the heat a little higher, but you'll have to monitor the onions more closely.

This works with any kind of onion, but Vidalia/sweet onions are traditional and yield the sweetest results. Don't panic if, at any point, it looks like they've burned. Add more liquid and give it a stir. That's how they get their beautiful caramel color!

"The research is really clear: plant-based food is the key to wellness and longevity. I enjoy feeling great and having lots of energy."

Spencer Harber
Spencer for Higher Wellness Coaching

Cashew Spread

serves 4-6

1 cup raw cashews (whole or pieces), soaked in warm water for at least 20 minutes and then strained
2 tablespoons nutritional yeast
1 garlic clove, peeled
Juice from ½ lemon
½ -¾ cup water
salt and pepper to taste

Add all of the ingredients EXCEPT water to your food processor or blender. Begin blending (scraping sides of your blender or food processor). Once mixture resembles course meal, slowly add water. Continue blending for 1-2 minutes. Check texture and repeat steps of adding water and blending until your spread resembles a thick hummus.

Serve as a dip, sandwich, or quesadilla spread, or stir into savory sauces to make them thick and creamy! Try blending in sundried tomatoes, spicy peppers, or other seasonings!

NOTES: If you're using a food processor vs. a high-powered blender, you'll want to let this run for several minutes to get the creamiest texture. Many people call this kind of recipe a cashew 'cheese,' but we think 'spread' is more accurate as it's closer to hummus than traditional cheese.

Eat within five days; we've found that it starts to taste stale after that.

Champagne Sauce

serves 4-6

¼ cup oil (vegetable or olive)
4-5 tablespoons vegan butter
dash of crushed red pepper (optional)
½ cup dry champagne or white wine (see notes)
1-2 cloves garlic, minced
1 shallot, minced (optional)
salt and pepper to taste
2-3 tablespoons fresh parsley (optional)

In a medium saucepan over medium high heat, melt oil and butter. Add crushed red pepper and garlic (and shallot, if using) and simmer for about a minute, being careful not to let it burn. Add champagne and continue simmering for 1-2 minutes. Both your butter and champagne will bubble - that's okay! (We've mistakenly browned both the shallots and butter and it's still delicious - you can see the color difference in the two photos!) Lastly, season to taste with salt and pepper and throw in fresh parsley (if using).

Pour over your favorite pasta or vegan protein (e.g., chick'n patties) and enjoy!

NOTES: Cooking with wine sounds fancy, but is so easy and adds such terrific flavor! Simply use your favorite, affordable wine. (If you'd drink it, it'll work in your recipe.)

You may also like a squeeze of fresh lemon juice or other herbs at the end. If you want to stretch it and/or play with the flavor, you can add vegetable broth or unsweetened plant-based milk (or both) after your wine has simmered. The sky's the limit! (...Almost. We haven't mastered an oil-free version yet; if you have, please tag us @plantbasedpoint and share your secret!)

Cheez Sauce

serves 6-8

2 potatoes, peeled and diced
3 carrots, peeled and diced
½ cup water
¾ cup nutritional yeast
½ cup vegetable broth
1 tablespoon lemon juice (about ½ lemon)
1 teaspoon salt
½ teaspoon garlic powder
½ teaspoon onion powder

Boil carrots and potatoes until fork tender, then drain. Add all ingredients to your blender (see notes) and blend until creamy.

Serve over nachos, as a potato topping, or whatever else you can dream up! Jules likes to stir soy chorizo and roasted broccoli in for a next-level soup.

NOTES: Depending on your blender, you may need to stop and scrape the sides and then continue blending. If you like a richer sauce and own a high-powered blender, try adding about ½ cup raw cashews, soaked in warm water for 20 minutes and then drained. (Add drained, soaked cashews to your blender when you add everything else.)

> "Ever since I was kid, you could find me wandering towards animals and plants (always being the kid coming home with dirt-covered feet at the end of the day). With this deep connection to animals and our mama Earth, I decided that I would help animals at the age of 5 and became a vegetarian when I was 11. Shortly after, I became vegan because it was one way I could be an advocate for things that don't have a voice."
>
> Kira Corbett
> Instagram @corbettkira

General Tso's Sauce

serves 2

4 tablespoons vinegar (rice, rice wine, apple cider, or white)
3 tablespoons soy sauce (can substitute tamari, dark soy, or low sodium)
3 tablespoons water or vegetable stock
4 tablespoons sugar (can substitute agave, maple syrup, or brown sugar)
1 tablespoons cornstarch (can substitute arrowroot)
1-2 cloves garlic, minced (see notes)
2 teaspoons ginger, minced (see notes)
1 tablespoon vegetable oil

FOR SESAME SAUCE, ADD:

1 teaspoon toasted sesame oil (or to taste)
2 teaspoons sesame seeds (or to taste)

OPTIONAL:

Scallions, sliced (for topping)
Crushed red pepper (to taste)

In a small bowl, whisk together all ingredients EXCEPT garlic, ginger, and oil. In a small saucepan over medium high heat, add oil and simmer garlic and ginger for 2-3 minutes (be careful not to burn garlic). Pour sauce mixture into saucepan and simmer until it begins to thicken, about 1-3 minutes.

Add any optional ingredients and enjoy over your favorite plant-based protein (we love fried tofu!), rice, and broccoli for that Chinese take-out experience without the regret (or cost!)!

NOTES: You can use dried garlic and ginger powder in place of fresh, but the end results won't have the same pop. If you're using garlic and ginger powder, you can simply add all ingredients in your bowl (including 1 tablespoon vegetable oil), whisk, and then simmer in small saucepan.

Mushroom Gravy

serves 6

8-10 ounces white or baby bella mushrooms, sliced
¼ cup vegan butter
¼ cup flour
4 cups vegetable or "no chick'n/beef" broth
salt and pepper to taste
Broth, water, or dry wine to deglaze (optional; see instructions)
Optional seasonings (dried or fresh): white pepper, thyme, sage, parsley, and/or rosemary to taste

In a medium saucepan over medium high heat, melt butter. Add mushrooms and simmer until well cooked (about 20 minutes). If you let the mushrooms begin to stick to the bottom of the pan (then add a splash of water, broth, or wine to loosen), your final result will be a rich, caramel-brown color and flavor.

Add flour and stir for 4-5 minutes (this will get rid of any flour flavor). Add 1 cup of broth and stir until it thickens. Add remaining broth, reduce heat, and simmer for about 30 minutes, until thickened. (Stir frequently.) Season to taste.

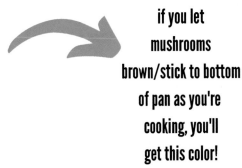

if you let mushrooms brown/stick to bottom of pan as you're cooking, you'll get this color!

NOTES: This recipe is relatively simple though time consuming, and well worth it. The final result is rich and flavorful and sure to please even the pickiest meat-lovers. Even better, it keeps wonderfully, meaning you can make it a day or two ahead and reheat before serving.

Peanut Sauce

serves 6

1 cup peanut butter (any kind - can substitute any nut or seed butter)
1 cup water (warmed if whisking by hand - see instructions)
½ cup soy sauce or tamari
½ cup agave
1 tablespoon fresh minced garlic
1 tablespoon fresh minced ginger
¼ cup chopped fresh cilantro (optional)
1-2 tablespoons fresh lemon or lime juice
1-2 teaspoons rice vinegar (can substitute white or apple cider)
1 tablespoon coconut aminos (optional)
crushed red pepper to taste (optional)

For Thai-style peanut satay sauce, add:
6-7 ounces full-fat coconut milk (or go crazy and use a whole 13.5-ounce can!)
1 tablespoon tomato paste
1-2 tablespoons fresh lime juice

Blend all ingredients in blender until smooth and creamy. (Note: if you blend in cilantro versus stirring it in afterwards, it'll throw off the color just slightly.)
-OR-
Using warm water, whisk all ingredients together in a medium-sized mixing bowl until blended.
-OR-
Simmer in a small saucepan over low to medium heat, stirring until blended. (Note: heating will cause sauce to thicken.)

Adjust as needed to taste (add more agave for sweeter sauce, more water for thinner sauce, etc.). Serve hot, cold, or room temperature over your favorite vegetables, grains, noodles, vegan protein, etc.!

NOTES: Will thicken in refrigerator. We like to make it on the thicker side, because once you add to noodles, and especially tofu or vegetables, it will thin out from the moisture in those ingredients.

Pumpkin Cream Sauce

serves 6

2-3 tablespoons vegan butter or oil (any kind)
1 white or yellow onion, chopped
1 15-ounce can pureed pumpkin
1 13.5-ounce can full-fat coconut milk
Salt and pepper to taste

In a large saucepan over medium high heat, heat butter or oil. Add onion and cook until translucent (5+ minutes). Add coconut milk, pumpkin, salt and pepper, and simmer for 5 minutes. If you like a silky smooth sauce, carefully transfer to a blender and purée.

You can eat as-is as a soup, serve over pasta, rice, or gnocchi topped with nutritional yeast, or turn into a stew. Some of our favorite stew add-ins are: black beans, plant-based sausage, spinach, sun-dried tomatoes, sage, and mushrooms. (If using mushrooms, cook them with onions until well done.)

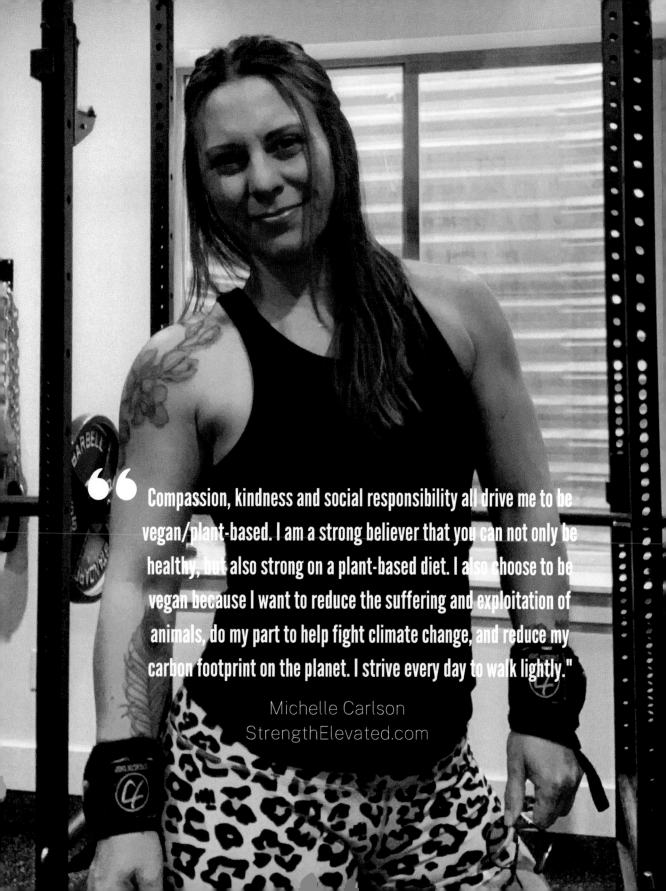

"Compassion, kindness and social responsibility all drive me to be vegan/plant-based. I am a strong believer that you can not only be healthy, but also strong on a plant-based diet. I also choose to be vegan because I want to reduce the suffering and exploitation of animals, do my part to help fight climate change, and reduce my carbon footprint on the planet. I strive every day to walk lightly."

Michelle Carlson
StrengthElevated.com

Ranch Dressing

serves 8

1 12-ounce package silken tofu (see notes)
¼ cup unsweetened, unflavored plant-based milk
2 teaspoons onion powder
1 teaspoon apple cider vinegar
2 teaspoons garlic powder
Sea salt and freshly ground black pepper to taste
3 tablespoons each of fresh dill and parsley
Fresh scallions or chives to taste

In a blender, add everything EXCEPT fresh herbs/chives. Blend until creamy and smooth. Transfer to a bowl. Stir in parsley, dill, and chives (or scallions). Adjust seasoning. Chill before serving. Thin with additional milk if needed.

NOTES: If you don't like the taste of tofu, refrigerate at least four hours before tasting and adjusting seasonings. You'll be amazed what happens to this dressing over time - it keeps getting better and you'd never know it was made with tofu!

" My vegan journey started when my husband was diagnosed with Rheumatoid arthritis at a very early age (36). He took medicine frequently to ease his daily hip and knee pain. We watched the documentary, "What The Health" and agreed to cut out meat and dairy from our diet. Within two months, Chris was completely off all pain medications and just last year completed his first marathon! Over the last four years we have learned more of the inhumane treatment of animals, and this has sparked a stronger belief that the vegan lifestyle is meant for us."

Kate Parente

" After being a heavy meat-eater for most of my life, I realized that there's simply no point, health-wise or ethically, for eating animals. Since I went 100% vegan five years ago, I've stopped contributing to factory farming and my body has never felt better!"

Eric Dubs

Sundried Tomato Pesto

serves 6-8

1 cup walnuts
4-5 ounces sundried tomatoes packed in oil (see notes)
2 cups arugula
¼-½ cup basil
1 tablespoon fresh lemon juice
1 small clove garlic, peeled
Salt and pepper to taste

Pop garlic clove into a food processor and pulse until minced (only takes a few seconds). Add remaining ingredients EXCEPT arugula and pulse until fairly well blended. Lastly, add arugula in batches, mixing until everything is blended.

In addition to going wonderfully with any pasta, this makes a fantastic quesadilla or wrap spread!

NOTES: This is a great way to make a hearty batch of pesto without breaking the bank on pine nuts - or when basil isn't in season!

If your pesto (whether it's this recipe or any other) ever has too much of a 'bite,' try reducing the fresh garlic, or substituting with roasted garlic, and increase the nutritional yeast and/or nuts.

To make this oil-free, purchase plain sundried tomatoes and soak in hot water until softened.

Tahini Italian Dressing

serves 6

½ cup tahini
½ cup unsweetened plant-based milk
1 clove raw garlic, peeled -AND/OR- 4-5 cloves roasted garlic (use either or both!)
1 tablespoon dried oregano
1 tablespoon dried basil
1 tablespoon balsamic or white wine vinegar -AND/OR- 1 tablespoon fresh lemon juice
Pinch of crushed red pepper (optional)
Salt and pepper to taste

In a small food processor (see notes), add garlic and pulse until minced. Add remaining ingredients and pulse until blended. Adjust seasonings to taste.

Make this a day ahead and store in an airtight container in the fridge, allowing the flavors to really come together! This continues to get better and better for several days and will thicken in refrigerator; simply add more plant-based milk to thin (if you prefer).

NOTES: If you don't have a food processor, simply mince your garlic ahead of time and whisk everything together in a small bowl.

> **"** I'm vegan for the animals and the planet. I don't want my eating habits to be the cause of unnecessary suffering when I can live my best life without animal products. One of my favorite quotes is by Philip Wollen: 'When it comes to suffering, a pig is a dog, is a bear, is a boy.'"
>
> Karin Bills

Tofu Ricotta

serves 8

1 12-14 ounce package firm or extra firm tofu, pressed (see notes)
1 clove garlic (minced if you're not using a food processor) -OR- 1 tablespoon garlic powder
¼ cup nutritional yeast
1-2 tablespoons fresh lemon juice
Salt and pepper to taste

Optional seasonings:
1 tablespoon dried oregano
2-3 cloves roasted garlic
1 tablespoon white miso paste
1 teaspoon crushed red pepper
Dried or fresh basil to taste
Olive oil to taste

If using a food processor (recommended, but a blender or hand mixer should also do the trick), place garlic clove inside and pulse until minced. Add tofu, nutritional yeast, lemon juice, salt and pepper (and any optional ingredients) and blend until you have a smooth, creamy texture. (You may need to scrape the sides of the bowl and then continue blending.)

Taste and adjust seasonings as desired. Use in all of your favorite Italian recipes (we recommend doubling for Lasagna [page 114]) or as a sandwich spread!

NOTES: See the 'Plant-Based Primer' section for our easy tofu pressing method!

Vodka Sauce

Great make-ahead dish!

serves 6-8

1 stick (½ cup) vegan butter
1 Vidalia onion, chopped
1 large can or jar (18-28 ounces) crushed tomatoes or plain tomato sauce
1 can (13.5-ounces) full-fat coconut milk
2-4 cloves garlic, minced
½ cup vodka
Salt and pepper to taste

In a large saucepan over medium high heat, melt butter. Add chopped onion and sauté until onions are translucent (5+ minutes). Add tomatoes and simmer for 5-10 minutes. Next, add garlic, vodka, and coconut milk and simmer for an additional 10-15 minutes (until vodka flavor dissipates). Season with salt and pepper.

Turn off heat and carefully transfer to your blender. Blend until smooth and creamy. Serve over your favorite pasta, plant-based chick'n, or Meatless Balls (page 33).

NOTES: This does NOT taste like coconut and is a very forgiving recipe. You can use a white or yellow onion, and more or less of any of the ingredients and still wind up with a delicious sauce. You can even skip the garlic and vodka and it'll taste good! The only trick is a bit of patience, letting each ingredient "get happy" (as Jules's sister says - and she helped develop this recipe!) once it enters your pot.

Soups, Salads + Sides

Broccoli Salad   81

Carrot-Ginger Soup 82

Chickpea Salad 83

Coleslaw 85

Creamed Greens 87

Fried Shallots Salad 88

Macaroni/Potato Salad 90

> " I am vegan for the environment and for the billions of animals who needlessly die every year to feed humans. Opt for compassion, live the vegan lifestyle."

Dylan Klein

Broccoli Salad

serves 4-6

Great
make-
ahead
dish!

4 cups broccoli florets
1 cup shredded vegan cheddar cheese
4-5 strips vegan bacon (cooked according to package), crumbled
¼ cup red onion, finely chopped
1 cup vegan mayonnaise
1 tablespoon red wine vinegar (see notes)
2 tablespoons agave
½ teaspoon each salt and pepper, or to taste

In a large mixing bowl, combine all ingredients. Bam! Done. Serve cold like the stone cold beefless cake that you are.

NOTES: White, apple cider, or white wine vinegar will also work well. Jersey Jules has a soft spot for red wine vinegar because it reminds her of the Italian subs she used to get with her dad.

Carrot-Ginger Soup

serves 6-8

2 white or yellow onions, chopped
3 tablespoons vegan butter or oil
2 pounds carrots, peeled and cut into large chunks (can use baby carrots)
3 tablespoons fresh ginger, minced
6 cups vegetable or "no chick'n" broth
½ cup vegan sour cream (optional)
Salt and pepper to taste

Heat vegan butter or oil in large pot over medium high heat. Add onions and cook until translucent (5+ minutes). Add ginger, carrots, and broth, and bring to a boil. Boil until carrots are fork tender (5-10+ minutes). Let it cool down and then transfer to a blender (you'll likely need to do this in two batches). Blend until smooth and creamy, then return to your pot and add vegan sour cream (if using) and salt and pepper.

Serve on its own or alongside your favorite toasted sandwich. (We like to spread Tofu Ricotta [page 76] on sprouted toast.) This freezes wonderfully!

For a delicious soup topping, try blending equal parts walnuts and nutritional yeast.

Chickpea Salad

serves 2

One can (14-16 ounces) chickpeas, drained, rinsed, and mashed
¼ cup vegan mayonnaise (or to taste)
¼ cup red bell pepper, chopped
¼ cup celery, chopped
2 tablespoons chopped dill pickles or relish
Salt and pepper to taste
Dried dill to taste (optional)

In a medium sized bowl, add all of your ingredients and stir to combine. Taste and adjust seasonings as desired.

Enjoy on a sandwich or with crackers. You can also turn into a 'melt' by adding vegan cheese and frying your sandwich on the stovetop!

NOTES: Other seasonings or veggies work well with this, too! We especially like corn, chives, and scallions.

"I'm vegan for the animals! These beautiful sentient beings are capable of feeling fear, pain, and love. It helps me sleep at night knowing that I'm not supporting an exploitive industry that profits from their unimaginable suffering. With so many incredible vegan food options, it's really a no-brainer!"

Stefanie McGilp
StefanieMcGilpRealEstate.com

Coleslaw

serves 4-6

1 12-ounce package coleslaw mix (chopped cabbage + shredded carrots)
½ cup vegan mayonnaise (or to taste)
1-2 tablespoons red wine or apple cider vinegar
½-1 teaspoon celery seeds (see notes)
1-2 teaspoons agave
¼-½ cup thinly sliced cucumber and/or scallions (optional)

Combine all ingredients in a large bowl and adjust as desired to taste. Enjoy with your favorite BBQ meal or as an awesome sandwich or wrap condiment.

NOTES: Celery seeds are KEY - they're worth buying just to make perfect coleslaw!

"My main reason for a change was for the environment. I saw what the meat and dairy industries were doing to the earth and felt compelled to do anything I could to help lessen the burden on our planet. Through the change to plant-based I have also found joy in the added benefits on my health as well as not harming animals."

Sara Lehman

Creamed Greens

serves 4

16 ounces spinach or kale (or combo), rinsed, dried, and roughly chopped
1 tablespoon oil, water, or vegetable broth
1 onion (any variety), finely chopped
2 cloves garlic, minced
⅓ cup tahini
⅓-½ cup unsweetened plant-based milk
Salt and pepper to taste

OPTIONAL:

1 tablespoon fresh lemon juice
1 tablespoon white miso paste
¼ teaspoon nutmeg
¼ teaspoon white pepper
Pinch crushed red pepper

In a large saucepan over medium high heat, heat oil (or water or broth). Add onions and simmer until translucent (5+ minutes). Add garlic and stir for a minute. And greens and cook until greens have wilted. Turn off heat and add tahini, milk, seasonings, and any optional ingredients. Mix until well combined.

Serve alongside your favorite vegan meal, or use as a pasta topping!

Fried Shallots Salad

serves 6

6 cups arugula
1 acorn squash (see instructions)
2 shallots, finely chopped
2-3 tablespoons flour
2-3 tablespoons oil (any kind)
¼ cup dried cranberries
¼ cup pepitas (shelled pumpkin seeds), toasted (and, if you prefer, salted - you can purchase them this way)
Salt and pepper to taste

Recommended dressing: See our Balsamic Marinade/Dressing recipe (page 50)!

Preheat oven to 425 degrees F. Cut open squash and scoop out seeds. Cut into evenly-sized wedges (leave skins on). On a large, oiled baking sheet, coat your squash with 1 tablespoon oil, and sprinkle with salt and pepper to taste. Arrange evenly and bake 15-20 minutes, until golden brown and fork tender.

While squash is roasting, heat 1-2 tablespoons oil in a frying pan. Toss your shallots with flour in a small bowl (add salt and pepper to taste if you'd like). Once oil has heated, fry your shallots until crispy (about 5 minutes).

Assemble your salad: In a large bowl, add arugula and top with roasted squash, pepitas, dried cranberries, and lastly, fried shallots.

NOTES: This is also delicious with peeled and roasted sweet potatoes or other squash. If you want to keep things simple and use an oil-free dressing, balsamic vinegar (or balsamic vinegar reduction) works wonderfully.

Macaroni/Potato Salad

serves 8

Dressing:

¼ cup red onion, finely chopped
¼ cup scallions, sliced
½ cup celery, finely chopped
3 tablespoons fresh dill, chopped
1 cup vegan mayonnaise (or to taste)

For macaroni salad:

1-pound package macaroni, cooked
2 teaspoons agave
¾-1 cup peas
2 teaspoons apple cider vinegar

For potato salad:

6-7 large yukon gold potatoes, cut into 1-inch cubes and boiled until fork tender (we like to leave the skins on, but feel free to peel before slicing and boiling)
2 teaspoons red wine vinegar
1-2 teaspoons dijon mustard

While pasta or potatoes are still warm, place in a large mixing bowl and add a big dollop of vegan mayonnaise. (This will keep pasta from sticking together, or make your potato salad extra flavorful and creamy.) Once cooled, mix in all of your other ingredients and adjust seasonings to taste. Both pasta and potatoes absorb a lot of mayonnaise, so you may want to add more before serving.

NOTES: Other yummy add-ins: Macaroni salad: shredded carrots, fresh parsley, and bell pepper. Potato salad: sweet relish. A little BBQ sauce or vegan bacon in either tastes great, too!

Roasted Cauliflower and Farro Salad

serves 6

4 cups cauliflower florets (1 large head)
3 tablespoons vegetable broth (for roasting)
1 cup grain farro
1 tablespoon lemon juice (½ lemon)
2 teaspoons dijon mustard
½ cup raisins or diced dates
2 tablespoons fresh mint, chopped
2 tablespoons sunflower seeds

Step 1: Roast cauliflower: Preheat oven to 425 degrees F. On a large baking sheet, toss your cauliflower florets in 3 tablespoons vegetable broth. Bake for 25 minutes.

Step 2: Prepare farro: In a medium-sized pot, combine 1 cup farro and 2 cups vegetable broth, simmer for 20 minutes or until farro is soft, drain excess liquid.

Step 3: In a large mixing bowl, add lemon, dijon mustard, raisins, and cooked farro; stir to combine. Add roasted cauliflower and stir. Lastly, add sunflower seeds and mint, and lightly toss.

Enjoy warm or cold.

Scalloped Potatoes

serves 8

2.5 pounds Yukon gold potatoes, washed & thinly sliced (we like to leave skins on!)
1 large Vidalia onion, peeled, quartered, and thinly sliced
1 13.5-ounce can full-fat coconut milk, whisked to remove some of the lumps
⅓ -½ cup flour (any kind)
Salt and pepper to taste

OPTIONAL:
2-4 tablespoons of vegan butter, cut into little pats or cubes
⅓-½ cup unsweetened plant-based milk
⅓-½ cup nutritional yeast
Other seasonings to taste, e.g., rosemary, curry powder, thyme, scallions, etc.

Preheat oven to 375 degrees F. In a large baking dish (9 x 13-inch or approximate), layer potatoes and onions, one thin layer at a time. In between each layer, sprinkle salt, pepper, 1-2 tablespoons flour, 1 tablespoon nutritional yeast (if using), and 1/2-1 tablespoon vegan butter (if using), dabbing the butter across the layer. Finish the final layer using potatoes.

Pour coconut milk over top (it's okay if it's a little lumpy!) and sprinkle with remaining nutritional yeast (if using). If you want to add plant-based milk, don't fill the dish more than ⅓ of the way up or your final result will be a little soupy (though still delicious).

Bake for 1 hour and 10 minutes, or until golden brown and fork tender.
Let stand for 10-15 minutes before serving. Can make this ahead and reheat before serving.

NOTES: If you have a mandolin, this will make slicing much easier! The side of a box grater will also do the trick. Your onion and potato slices should be roughly 1/16-inch thick, but there's a bit of wiggle room! You can also use an 8x8-inch square baking dish, but may need to increase the cook time because your dish will be thicker.

This is a shockingly delicious, crowd-pleasing, and forgiving recipe. We've made it without vegan milk, butter, AND flour it's still so tasty. A great option for a non-vegan crowd, and does not taste like coconut!

Strawberry Basil Salad

serves 4-6

16 ounces strawberries, sliced
¼ of one red onion, thinly sliced
¼ cup fresh basil, chopped
¼-⅓ cup balsamic vinegar

In a large bowl, combine all ingredients. Taste and adjust as needed (you might prefer more basil and red onion). This is delicious right away, and flavors continue to enhance if refrigerated overnight.

Brighten up your summer BBQ, or bring summer into your kitchen any time of year, with this delicious, colorful, and healthy dish! You can also swap basil for mint and use as a topping for vegan vanilla ice cream or shortcake!

"Vegan for animals, to end their suffering and allow them a beautiful life on this planet."

Ericka Rodriguez
Axiology

Stuffing

serves 8

1 loaf (9-10 ounces) French or Italian bread, cut into cubes
(optional: leave on counter for 1-2 days to dry out)
1 stick (½ cup) vegan butter
½-¾ cup vegetable or "no chick'n" broth
3-4 celery stalks, diced
1 white or yellow onion, diced
8 ounces baby bella mushrooms, diced
1 small apple (any variety), peeled and diced
½-¾ cup walnuts or pecans, chopped (optional: toast)
1-2 tablespoons fresh sage, minced
2-4 tablespoons fresh parsley, minced
Salt and pepper to taste

Preheat oven to 425 degrees F (see notes). In a large saucepan over medium high heat, melt butter. Add onions and simmer until translucent (5+ minutes).

Add celery and cook for 2-3 minutes. Next, add mushrooms and fully cook. (10-15 minutes. You can put a lid on the pot to speed up process.) Add apples, sage, and parsley, and cook until apples just begin to soften (3-4 minutes).

Add nuts and bread, giving your mixture a good stir. Turn off heat. Lastly, stir in vegetable broth until bread is just moistened - you don't want it to become soggy.

Taste and add/adjust seasonings as needed. Transfer to a 9x13-inch (or similar) baking dish and bake for 20-30 minutes or until top is lightly toasted.

NOTES: You can use more bread without needing to add more vegetables and nuts; you'll simply use a little more vegetable broth (and vegan butter, if you'd like). You can cook this at a lower oven temperature if you're baking other things at the same time.

You can make this a day ahead: cover and refrigerate in your baking dish, and simply bake just before you're ready to serve. (Cook time may increase since dish will be cold.)

> " I love so many non-human species and don't want to contribute to their exploitation. For me, being vegan is easy and purposeful!"

Alyssa Almond
Certified Professional Coach
MWP Coaching

Summery Vegetable Sauté

serves 6

3 tablespoons oil (any kind)
1 onion (any variety), chopped
2 large zucchini, quartered and sliced into large chunks
1 cup cherry tomatoes, halved
1 cup corn (fresh really makes this dish pop)
2 cloves garlic, minced
¼ cup fresh basil, chopped
Salt and pepper to taste
Splash of balsamic vinegar (optional)

In a large saucepan over medium high heat, heat oil. Add onion and cook until translucent (5+ minutes). Next, add zucchini and cook until it begins to soften. (About 10 minutes.) If you let the zucchini begin to stick to the bottom of your pan (then add a splash of water or broth), you'll get a beautiful caramel color and flavor.

Add tomatoes and corn and cook another 1-2 minutes. Lastly, add basil, garlic, salt, pepper, and balsamic vinegar (if using) and cook 1-2 minutes until all of the flavors come together.

Serve hot or cold alongside your main dish, or on top of pasta!

Tortellini Vegetable Soup

serves 6

½ yellow onion, chopped
2 cloves garlic, minced
1 bag (12 ounces) frozen mixed vegetables
1 stalk celery, chopped
¼ cup water for sautéing
2 cans (28 ounces) diced tomatoes (no salt added)
3 cups vegetable broth
3 potatoes, diced (peeled if preferred)
1 package (about 9 ounces) non-dairy tortellini noodles
1 bay leaf
½ teaspoon each thyme, basil, oregano, and parsley
Salt and pepper to taste

In a large pot or saucepan, add ¼ cup water and bring to medium heat. Add onion and garlic and sauté for 5 minutes. Add in spices (except salt and pepper) and celery, stirring to combine. Add in frozen vegetables and stir.

Add diced tomatoes with juice, vegetable broth, and diced potatoes. Stir to combine, bring to boil, and add bay leaf.

Return to simmer for 25 minutes. Next, add tortellini and boil for 4 minutes (check after 2-3 minutes). Lastly, add salt and pepper to taste.

NOTES: This soup does not freeze well with tortellini (you could freeze the base and add tortellini before serving). Speaking of, be careful when cooking the tortellini; if they cook too long, they'll be mushy, and nobody wants a mushy noodle... (That's what we said.)

Whipped Sweet Potatoes

serves 6-8

5-6 sweet potatoes, roasted until skins begin to fall away (see notes)
1 large shallot (about 1/4 cup), minced
1 stick (½ cup) vegan butter
½-1 cup unsweetened plant-based milk
Salt and pepper to taste
Dried or fresh sage to taste (optional)

In a small frying pan over medium heat, simmer shallots in vegan butter until they soften, being very careful not to toast/burn.

Remove roasted sweet potatoes from skins and compost skins (or make your dog's day!). Using a food processor or hand mixer, blend together all ingredients EXCEPT plant-based milk. Slowly add milk until your desired consistency is reached. The longer you blend, the fluffier and more whipped it will become, which is a real crowd-pleaser!

Adjust seasonings to taste and serve alongside your favorite meals.

NOTES: This is a very simple recipe that packs a ton of flavor. Roasting the potatoes guarantees an extra rich, fantastic depth. (And Jules thinks it's easier than cutting and boiling; plus you can do other prep while they're in the oven!) Usually one hour at 425 degrees F will do the trick.

Zucchini Casserole

serves 6-8

2 tablespoons vegan butter or oil (any kind)
2 medium yellow squash, sliced into half moons or diced
2 medium zucchini squash, sliced into half moons or diced
1 onion (any variety), diced
¼-½ cup vegan mayonnaise
2-3 tablespoons fresh basil, minced
1-2 cloves garlic, minced
salt and pepper to taste

Topping:
1 sleeve vegan 'butter' crackers (~25 crackers), crushed
2 tablespoons vegan butter, melted

Preheat oven to 425 degrees F. In a large saucepan over medium high heat, melt butter or oil. Add onion and cook until translucent (5+ minutes). Add zucchini and yellow squash and cook until softened (10-15 minutes). Add garlic and basil and cook, stirring frequently, for 2-3 minutes (make sure garlic doesn't burn).

Turn off heat and stir in mayonnaise, salt, and pepper. Adjust to taste and pour into an 8x8-inch or 9x13-inch (or similar) baking dish.

Prepare your topping by combining crushed crackers and melted butter in a bowl or food processor. Sprinkle over top of your zucchini dish and bake for 15 minutes or until golden brown and bubbly.

Let stand for 10-15 minutes before serving.

NOTES: Feel free to use all yellow squash or all green zucchini in this dish. You can use a cashew cream, tahini + plant-based milk, or silken tofu in place of mayonnaise. This is a popular Thanksgiving dish, and using fresh basil really makes it stand out from the traditional holiday fare!

Main Courses

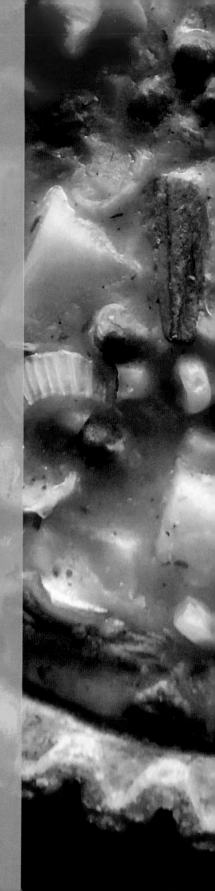

Breakfast Burritos

yields 4-6 extra-stuffed (or up to 10 lightly-stuffed) burritos

1 10-count package large (burrito size) tortillas
1 package (12-14 ounces) firm or extra firm tofu, pressed
¼ cup vegetable broth
2 cloves garlic, minced
½ yellow onion, chopped
1 red bell pepper, chopped
1 package (32 ounces) diced or shredded hash browns (will yield extra hash browns)

Hash brown seasoning:

1 tablespoon nutritional yeast
1 teaspoon smoked paprika
½ teaspoon garlic powder
½ teaspoon onion powder
Salt and pepper to taste

Tofu/vegetable seasoning:

½ teaspoon garlic powder
½ teaspoon onion powder
1 teaspoon turmeric
Salt and pepper to taste

Preheat oven to 350 degrees F. Press tofu if you've not already done so. (For tips on tofu pressing, see our 'Plant-Based Primer' section.)

In a large frying pan over medium high heat, add vegetable broth. Next, add garlic, onion, and red bell pepper. Cook until onions are translucent (5+ minutes).

In another large frying pan, cook hash browns according to package instructions. Add nutritional yeast, smoked paprika, garlic powder, onion powder, and salt and pepper to taste.

Crumble tofu and add to your pan with garlic, onion, and bell pepper. Season with garlic powder, onion powder, turmeric, and salt and pepper to taste. Cook this mixture for about 5 minutes or until tofu is warm throughout.

Now you're ready to assemble your burritos! Grab a 9x13 inch baking dish or one suitable to fit 4-6 large, or up to 10 small, burritos (depending how full you like them). Fill each tortilla evenly with the tofu/veggie mix and the hash brown mix. Fold into a burrito shape and place inside baking dish. (Pro tip: push as many burritos as possible together to help keep their shape.)

Bake for 20 mins or until edges start to brown. If you're enjoying later, let them cool, then wrap in foil and put in fridge or freezer. If you want a real burrito party, try topping with our warmed cheez sauce (page 59)!

Burrito Folding 101

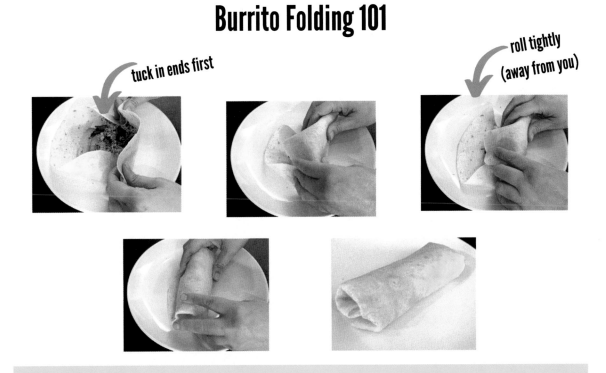

tuck in ends first

roll tightly (away from you)

NOTES: For this recipe, we prefer to freeze the tofu and set in the refrigerator to thaw the night before we plan to use - it cuts down on the pressing process and adds a heartier, chewier texture.

"Butter" Tofu

serves 8

1 16-ounce package extra firm, high-protein tofu, water squeezed out, sliced into bite-sized cubes
2 tablespoons oil (any kind)
1 large white or yellow onion, chopped
4 cloves garlic, minced
2 teaspoons fresh ginger, minced
1 28-ounce can crushed tomatoes or plain tomato sauce
1 ½ cups raw cashews, soaked in warm water
1 ½ cups unsweetened plant-based milk
2 tablespoons brown sugar
Salt and pepper to taste
Fresh cilantro (optional)

Spice mix:
1 tablespoon garam masala
2 teaspoons ground cumin
1 tablespoon curry powder
2 teaspoons paprika
1 teaspoon ground coriander
1 teaspoon ground turmeric

In a small dish, combine spice mix. Set aside. In a large pan over medium high heat, add oil and sauté onions until translucent (5+ minutes). Add garlic, ginger, and spice mix. Stir for 1-2 minutes, until fragrant. Add crushed tomatoes (or tomato sauce).

While tomatoes simmer, strain cashews and place in blender. Add plant-based milk to blender and blend together until smooth and creamy. Pour into a dish/measuring cup and set aside. Don't clean the blender yet, because next you'll carefully pour your tomato mixture into your blender and blend until smooth.

Return the blended tomato mixture to pan and pour in cashew cream. Bring to a light simmer and add tofu. Next, add brown sugar and stir to dissolve. Continue to lightly simmer for about 5-10 minutes. Add salt and pepper and adjust seasonings to taste.

Cashew Alfredo

serves 6-8

1 ½ cups raw cashews (whole or pieces), soaked in warm water for at least 20 minutes
2 cups unsweetened plant-based milk
1 medium onion, any variety, roughly chopped (see notes)
½ cup nutritional yeast or vegan parmesan cheese
2 cloves garlic, peeled
2 tablespoons fresh lemon juice
1 tablespoon white miso paste (optional)
Salt and pepper to taste

Place all ingredients in blender and blend for at least two minutes until smooth and creamy. Adjust flavors and add more plant-based milk as needed.

Serve warm over your favorite pasta and/or roasted vegetables.

NOTES: If you're using a food processor or lower-powered blender, either soak your cashews overnight or simmer in a small saucepan for about 30 minutes until they're extremely soft.

For the richest flavor, first cook your onions by sautéing in oil over medium high heat until they begin to slightly brown (about 10 minutes).

❝ As a kid, there was nothing I loved more than animals and nature. When I learned how catastrophic the meat industry is not just for the animals trapped in it, but for the planet and even for our bodies, I didn't see any other logical solution than to take meat off my plate. Going vegan has felt like opening up my whole heart, living in alignment with my deepest values, and truly thriving."

Shawna Weaver
Founder, Blue Sky Alchemy
BlueSkyAlchemy.co

Garlicky Pasta

serves 4

EASY assembles & cooks in one pot!

¼ cup water for sautéing
1 cup unsweetened plant-based milk
2 cups vegetable broth
4 garlic cloves, minced
1 tablespoon vegan butter
Salt and pepper to taste
8 ounces pasta (linguini, fettuccine, spaghetti, or penne), uncooked
Parsley (fresh or dried) and nutritional yeast for topping

Add ¼ cup water to large saucepan or pot and warm to medium high heat. Add garlic and sauté for 2 minutes. Once warmed, add vegan butter, salt, and pepper and sauté for 2-3 minutes. Pour in non-dairy milk and vegetable broth, add uncooked pasta, and turn heat to high.

Bring to a boil, then turn down to simmer, and allow to simmer for 15 minutes or until most of liquid is absorbed by noodles and they're cooked to your liking (time can vary depending on noodle choice).

Sprinkle with parsley (fresh or dried) and nutritional yeast, and dig in! Pairs well with your favorite veggies, our Fried Shallots Salad (page 88), or Summery Vegetable Sauté (page 99).

Lasagna

serves 8

1 9-ounce package no-boil lasagna noodles (see notes)
2 24-ounce jars of your favorite tomato sauce or single
batch of vodka sauce (page 77)
Double batch of tofu ricotta (page 76)
1 cup crumbled plant-based meat or sausage (optional)
1 onion (any variety), chopped
1-2 garlic cloves, minced
1 cup your favorite veggies, chopped (optional)
1-2 tablespoons olive oil and/or water for sautéing
½ cup nutritional yeast (optional: blend with 1/2 cup walnuts for a nice crunch!)
1 8-ounce bag of shredded vegan mozzarella (optional)

Preheat oven to 375 degrees F (or refer to lasagna box instructions).

Heat oil and/or water in a large frying pan and cook onion until translucent (5+ minutes).
Add any other veggies and cook until they begin to soften. Add garlic and vegan meat (if
using) and sauté until meat begins to brown (if just using garlic, stir for 1-2 minutes until
fragrant). Turn off heat and add tomato sauce (you may have to transfer to a bowl if your
pan isn't large enough).

Follow pasta box instructions to assemble and bake your lasagna or:

Spread ⅕ of sauce/veggie/meat mixture on the bottom of a 9x13 dish. Next add one layer
of pasta noodles (= 3 noodles). Before placing noodles in pan, spread tofu ricotta on each
one, then lay them in pan (ricotta side up). Sprinkle ¼ of nutritional yeast and shredded
mozzarella (if using) on top. Pour ⅕ of tomato sauce mixture over cheese(s), and continue
layering in the same order.

When you reach the final (top) layer of pasta noodles, top with remaining tomato sauce
(be sure to cover the noodles so they'll cook properly), nutritional yeast, and shredded
cheese.

Bake for 35-40 minutes and then let stand for at least 20 minutes before serving. This
recipe freezes really well (and some might argue tastes better over the following days!).

made with Vodka Sauce (page 77)!

NOTES: Lasagna is labor intensive, but so worth the effort. It makes such a hearty amount and freezes well, so your work will not be in vain! Once you're comfortable with the basics, you can start experimenting with all kinds of fillings and sauces.

Many lasagna noodles contain eggs, so be sure to check the labels. You can certainly use regular lasagna noodles that you boil before assembling, but this adds an extra step and makes it much harder to spread tofu ricotta. We've tried it both ways and think no-boil noodles taste just as delicious! Added bonus: this is the only recipe where Jules has used whole wheat (no boil) pasta noodles and not noticed a difference in taste!

Mung Bean Curry

serves 4

1 cup cooked mung beans (see notes)
2-3 tablespoons water or oil (any kind)
2 medium onions (any variety), chopped
2-3 tablespoons fresh ginger, minced
3-4 cloves garlic, minced
1 can (13.5-ounces) full-fat coconut milk
Salt and pepper to taste

Never had mung beans? They taste like a cross between a split pea and lentil and we absolutely love them! You can often find them in the bulk section or where dried flours and beans are sold.

OPTIONAL:

8-12+ ounces fresh greens, rinsed and roughly chopped (e.g., spinach, bok choy, collard greens, etc.)
2-4+ tablespoons soy sauce
2-4+ tablespoons coconut aminos
Crushed red pepper to taste

In a large saucepan over medium high heat, add oil or water and sauté onions until translucent (5+ minutes). Add garlic and ginger and sauté for 2-3 minutes, then add cooked mung beans and stir for 1-2 minutes.

Pour in can of coconut milk and simmer for 5-15 minutes until it begins to thicken. Add other optional ingredients (if using) and adjust to taste. Serve warm as-is or over your favorite rice.

NOTES: To cook mung beans yielding one cup, in a small saucepan simmer ½ cup dried, rinsed mung beans with 1 ½ cups water or broth for about 30-40 minutes, or until softened. Drain any excess liquid.

If you prefer a soupier curry, you can simply cut back on mung beans or add an extra can of coconut milk!

Pot Pie

yields two bottom crust-only pies

2 pie crusts (see notes)
1 yellow onion, diced
1 clove garlic, minced
1 medium potato (any variety), peeled and diced
2 carrots, peeled and diced
2 celery stalks, diced
1 10-ounce (about 1 cup) bag frozen green beans or peas
1 10-ounce (about 1 cup) bag frozen corn
1 15.5-ounce can cannellini beans (or your favorite bean!), drained and rinsed

Black pepper, thyme, and nutritional yeast to taste

Filling:
¼ cup flour
2 cups vegetable broth
1 cup unsweetened plant-based milk

Preheat oven to 400 degrees F. Warm a large frying pan over medium heat and add about 1 tablespoon vegetable broth from your 2 cups. Add garlic, celery, and onions and cook until broth begins to absorb.

Next, add carrots, green beans or peas, corn, beans, broth, plant-based milk, and flour and stir to combine. Bring to a boil and then return to medium low, simmering for 8 minutes.

Add dried thyme, pepper, and nutritional yeast to taste and continue mixing. (We like a dash of pepper, about 1 tablespoon nutritional yeast, and 1 teaspoon thyme.)

When ready, scoop your mixture into your pie crusts. Bake for 45 min. Let stand for 5-15 minutes before serving. These freeze wonderfully!

NOTES: For this recipe, we use two pre-made, frozen pie crusts that are vegan-friendly (many are!) and use only a bottom crust for each pie. The crusts remain in the freezer until it's time to bake, cutting down on prep time!

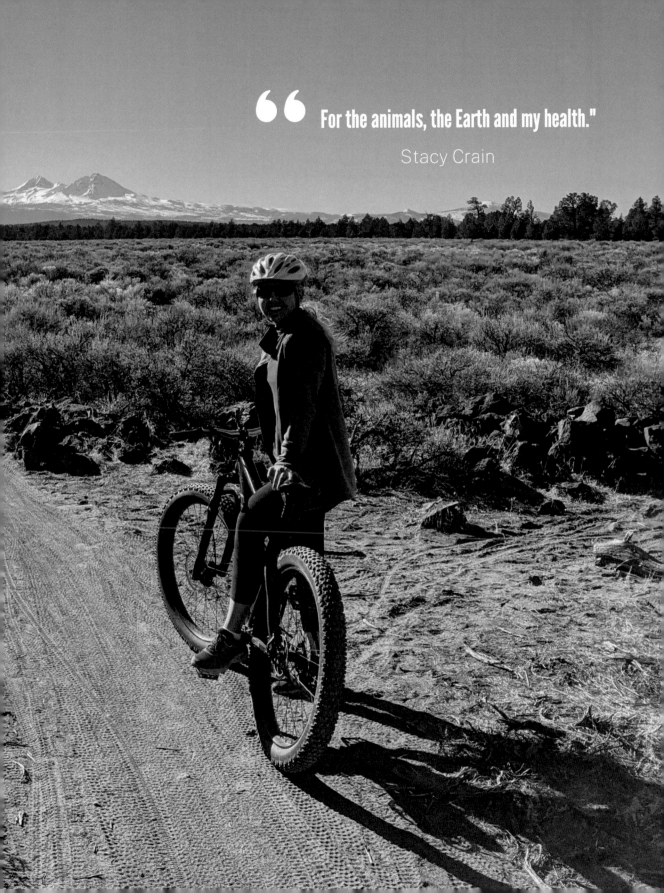

" For the animals, the Earth and my health."

Stacy Crain

Red Wine-Mushroom Sauce with Beefless Tips

serves 2

1 onion (any variety), chopped
2 tablespoons vegan butter
2 tablespoons oil (any kind)
1 shallot, minced
1-2 cloves garlic, minced
½ cup red wine (see notes)
2 portabella mushrooms, sliced or diced
1 (9-ounce) bag beefless tips
Salt and pepper to taste
Fresh parsley or scallions, chopped, to garnish (optional)
Water or vegetable broth to deglaze pan (optional - see instructions)

In a large pan over medium high heat, melt butter and oil. Add onion and cook until translucent (5+ minutes). Add mushrooms, put lid on pan, and cook down for about 10 minutes. (Add a splash of water or broth throughout if things stick to the bottom of the pan too much - a little bit will get you a nice caramelization.)

Add beefless tips and cook for about 5 minutes. Add shallots and garlic and cook for an additional 2 minutes, stirring frequently (don't let them burn!). Add red wine and continue cooking down until most of the liquid is absorbed - about 2-3 minutes. Season with salt and pepper to taste.

NOTES: Cooking with wine sounds fancy, but is so easy and adds such terrific flavor! Simply use your favorite, affordable wine. (If you'd drink it, it'll work in your recipe.)

Spanakopita Pie

yields 8 large pieces

For filling:

2-3 tablespoons olive oil
2 onions (any variety), chopped
4 cloves garlic, minced
2-3 tablespoons fresh lemon juice
½ cup fresh parsley, chopped
2 teaspoons dried dill
2 teaspoons dried oregano
2 14-ounce packages extra firm tofu, pressed and crumbled (see notes)
8 ounces spinach or baby spinach, chopped (see notes)
4 ounces vegan cream cheese
Salt and pepper to taste

For pastry layers:

1 stick vegan butter, melted (see notes)
1 16-ounce package phyllo pastry sheets, thawed (see notes)

To make the filling: In a large pan over medium high heat, add olive oil. Add onions and cook until translucent (5+ minutes). Add garlic and herbs and stir for 1-2 minutes, until fragrant. Add tofu and spinach and cook until spinach has wilted (usually a couple of minutes). Turn off heat and add cream cheese (feel free to use more!). Add salt and pepper and adjust seasonings to taste. Don't be shy - this recipe can withstand A LOT of flavor once wrapped up in a light phyllo sandwich!

To assemble the pie: Preheat oven to 325 degrees F. Lightly grease a 9x13-inch baking dish. Unwrap your thawed phyllo and place it between two damp cloths to keep from drying out while you assemble your dish. Take two phyllo sheets and place on the bottom of your baking dish. (It's okay if it folds over the sides of your dish.) Brush with about 1 tablespoon melted vegan butter - just enough to coat the layer. Repeat, two sheets at a time, until you've used ⅔ of the sheets. Don't worry if the sheets split or break!

Pour your filling into your dish and spread until it's even. Continue layering phyllo sheets and coating with butter, two sheets at a time, until you've run out of phyllo sheets. (A typical phyllo package has about 17 phyllo sheets, so we like to use 11 on the bottom and 6 on top.

Fold the edges inward (roughly resembling pie crust) and coat the top and edges with remaining butter. Taking a sharp knife, cut halfway through the sheets into eight large squares. Cut until you reach the filling, but DON'T cut all the way to the bottom. (This will make it much easier to slice the final pie.)

Bake until golden brown - about 1 hour to 1 hour and 20 minutes. Let stand for 10-15 minutes before serving. It will stay crispy for several hours - and is still delicious leftover, just not as crispy!

NOTES: Most frozen phyllo dough is "accidentally vegan" - just check for butter. Also check your phyllo package regarding thawing instructions. Usually they recommend thawing in the fridge overnight, so you want to plan ahead.

You can substitute olive oil for vegan butter to layer your phyllo sheets, but we find that the butter makes it flakier. You don't need a brush to coat your layers - Jules just uses a spoon!

We love using fresh spinach for this recipe, but you can certainly use frozen. Thaw first and squeeze out extra water.

You can make your filling a day or two ahead if you'd like. If you want to keep things simple, you can skip the phyllo and enjoy this filling inside a tortilla or with some toast as a flavorful breakfast scramble!

For tofu pressing tips, see the 'Plant-Based Primer' section.

Thai Curry

serves 2-3

1 13.5-ounce can full-fat coconut milk
1 4-ounce jar or tin of your favorite curry paste (see notes)
⅓-½ cup water (optional)
½ medium white or yellow onion, chopped
½ bell pepper (any color), chopped
1 8-ounce can bamboo shoots, drained and rinsed
1 cup broccoli or cauliflower florets, rinsed
½-¾ cup tofu, drained and cubed (see notes)

OTHER VEGGIE IDEAS:
1-2 potatoes, cubed
Green beans
Snow peas
Mushrooms, sliced
Water chestnuts
Carrots, sliced

OPTIONAL TOPPINGS/ADD-INS:
½-1 cup water
Thai basil
Cilantro
Scallions
Spicy peppers/hot sauce (e.g., crushed red pepper)

In a medium saucepan over medium high heat, sauté onion in curry paste until the onion begins to soften (3-5 minutes). Add bell pepper and continue cooking until pepper begins to soften (3-5 minutes). Pour in coconut milk and stir until blended. For thinner curry, add ½-1 cup of water. Add broccoli and/or cauliflower and simmer for a minute. Finally, add bamboo shoots and tofu and simmer until vegetables are softened to your liking.

Turn off heat and stir in any optional toppings/add-ins. Enjoy on its own or over jasmine rice!

NOTES: If you like milder curry, you can use two cans of coconut milk per one can of curry paste. Check your curry paste instructions as some recommend you use only 1-2 tablespoons per can of coconut milk.

If playing around with veggies, add them to the coconut milk mixture according to the length of time they need to cook. Always start with the onions and cook until they begin to soften. If you're using potatoes or mushrooms, they'll require longer cooking, so add them next (after onion). Broccoli generally takes the least amount of time and is the least forgiving (quickly going from crisp to soggy).

Desserts

Almond Butter Cups 131

Chocolate Cupcakes with
Chocolate Avocado Frosting 132

Chocolate Mousse Truffles 134

Ginger Beer Bread 136

Peanut Butter Chocolate
Cereal Bars 138

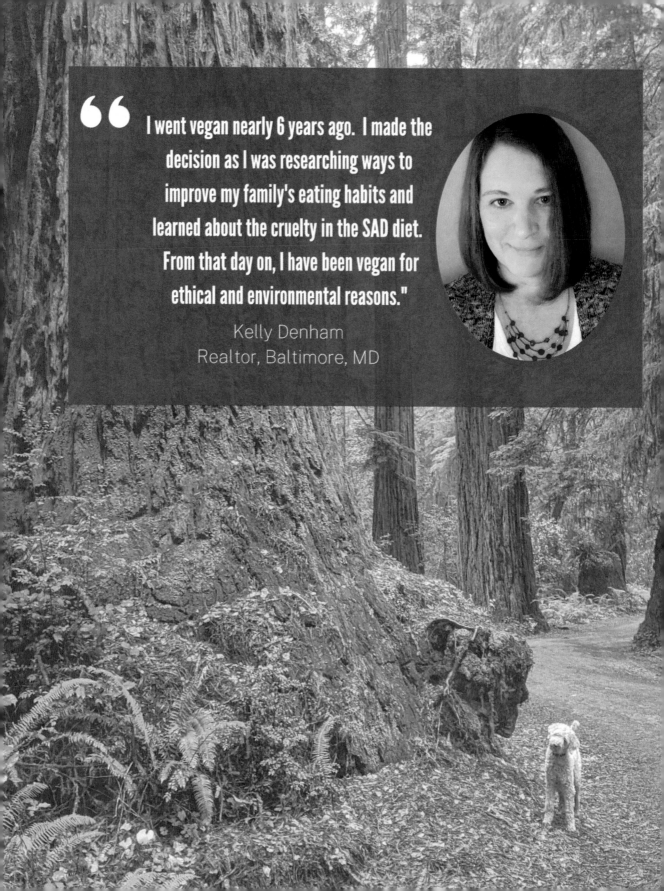

> "I went vegan nearly 6 years ago. I made the decision as I was researching ways to improve my family's eating habits and learned about the cruelty in the SAD diet. From that day on, I have been vegan for ethical and environmental reasons."

Kelly Denham
Realtor, Baltimore, MD

Almond Butter Cups

yields 24 "cups"

12 dates, sliced in half and pitted
½ cup almond butter (see notes)
½ cup raisins
Dash of cinnamon and Celtic salt

Scoop about ½ tablespoon almond butter into the center of each pitted date half. Add a few raisins, a sprinkle of cinnamon, and dash of Celtic salt. Once your cups are assembled, refrigerate for at least one hour, then serve and enjoy!

NOTES: You can swap out almond butter with any nut or seed butter. You can also add crushed nuts, non-dairy chocolate chips, or whatever toppings sound good to you!

Chocolate Cupcakes with Chocolate Avocado Frosting

yields 12-18 cupcakes (see notes)

Cupcakes:

1 ½ cups all-purpose flour
1 cup sugar
¼ cup unsweetened cocoa powder
1 teaspoon baking soda
½ teaspoon salt
1 cup water
⅓ cup vegetable oil
1 tablespoon apple cider vinegar
1 teaspoon vanilla
1 cup vegan chocolate chips or mini chips (optional)

Frosting:

1 cup (about 2 medium) ripe avocados, peeled and pits removed (see notes)
1 tablespoon vanilla
⅓ cup cocoa powder
3 ½ cups powdered sugar
½ teaspoon salt
3 tablespoon plant-based milk

Preheat oven to 350 degrees F and lightly grease a 12-count cupcake tin (or line with cupcake liners), including the top of the cupcake pan because your cupcakes will spill over slightly. In a large mixing bowl, combine cupcake dry ingredients (flour, sugar, cocoa powder, baking soda, and salt).

Make a well in the center of your dry ingredients and add water, vegetable oil, vinegar, and vanilla. Stir until combined. Next, stir in vegan chocolate chips (if using - we highly recommend!). Fill cupcake tins nearly full and bake for 20-30 minutes, or until a knife inserted in center comes out clean.

While cupcakes are cooking, add avocados and vanilla to a large bowl. Using a hand or stand mixer, beat for 1-2 minutes. Add half of the cocoa powder, powdered sugar, and salt and beat until well mixed. Add the remaining cocoa powder, sugar, and salt and beat until fully mixed. (You may need to scrape the sides of the bowl with a rubber spatula throughout.) Lastly, add the plant-based milk and blend.

Once cupcakes have completely cooled, frost. (Optional: sprinkle extra chocolate chips on top!)

NOTES: You can swap out avocados with two sticks (1 cup) of softened vegan butter. For best results, make sure you beat butter until it's light and fluffy before adding powdered sugar (butter should be room temperature, not melted). You can easily turn this into a cream cheese frosting by adding 8 ounces vegan cream cheese and enough additional powdered sugar to reach a light and fluffy consistency.

If you prefer smaller cupcakes, you can fill your cupcake tins halfway and this will yield about 18 cupcakes.

Chocolate Mousse Truffles

yields 30+ truffles

2 10-ounce bags dairy-free chocolate chips
1 13.5-ounce can coconut cream
½ cup cashew butter (see notes)
2 tablespoons cocoa powder
1 tablespoon vegan butter
1 teaspoon vanilla extract
⅛ teaspoon salt

Optional additions: ½ cup nuts, crushed vegan cookies, or 1 tsp mint or almond extract

Mousse filling: Place 10 ounces chocolate chips, cashew butter, and coconut cream in a microwave safe container. Microwave in 30 second intervals, stirring in between, until melted and blended (usually 90-120 seconds). See notes for alternative melting method.

Transfer to food processor or large mixing bowl and stir in cocoa powder, vanilla and salt. Stir in any optional ingredients.

Pour into an 8x8-inch (or approximate) baking dish and freeze for at least one hour, or refrigerate for at least four hours, until set. Cut into bite-sized pieces or roll into balls.

Chocolate coating: Place 10 ounces chocolate chips + 1 tablespoon vegan butter in a microwave safe container and melt using method above. Line a baking sheet with wax paper. Coat your fudge pieces in melted chocolate and place on wax paper. Place in freezer or refrigerator until set. Store leftover pieces in an airtight container in the refrigerator.

NOTES: If you don't have a microwave, you can melt/blend topping together over the stovetop using the double boiler method. (See 'Peanut Butter Chocolate Cereal Bars' on page 138.)

Cashew butter is used here for texture, not taste. If you swap out or omit it, your filling will not be as firm, but is still delicious! You can also pour this mousse filling into a pre-baked pie shell for a rich and delicious no-bake chocolate cream pie!

Ginger Beer Bread

serves 8

3 cups all-purpose flour
1 tablespoon baking powder
1 teaspoon salt
¼ cup sugar
12 ounces ginger beer
¼-½ cup vegan butter, melted

Preheat oven to 375 degrees F. Grease a loaf pan or 8x8-inch baking dish. Combine all ingredients EXCEPT vegan butter in a large mixing bowl and transfer to your baking dish. Pour melted vegan butter over top (this gives the top a nice buttery crunch).

Bake for about 40-60 minutes (depending on pan size - loaf takes longer) or until a knife inserted in center comes out clean.

NOTES: We put this under the dessert category because it's delightfully sweet, but not overpoweringly so, and could also pair well with certain dinners, like chili or BBQ night.

" Vegan for the animals! I stopped eating animals in 1980, and believe me, it wasn't as easy as it is now! Since dairy farm abuse wasn't well-known then, I ate a lot of dairy; also bought a lot of cookbooks. Finding out about the environmental and health benefits was a bonus! Have now been vegan for about six years, and wish I'd done it earlier."

Jeanne Leigh

Peanut Butter Chocolate Cereal Bars

yields 12 bars

1 cup light corn syrup
1 cup sugar
1 cup peanut butter
7 cups rice or corn flake cereal
2 cups vegan chocolate chips
1 stick (½ cup) vegan butter

Lightly grease a 9-x13-inch (or approximate) baking dish. Set aside.

In a large pot over medium heat, melt together corn syrup and sugar until sugar dissolves. Turn off heat and stir in peanut butter. Next, stir in cereal. Transfer cereal mixture to greased dish, pressing lightly until it's evenly spread throughout pan.

In microwave, melt together chocolate chips and butter until completely melted. Start with 30 seconds, and continue stirring and checking every 20-30 seconds (should take 90-120 seconds overall). It's very easy to burn chocolate, turning it into a lumpy, bitter mess, so don't rush this step! For an alternative melting method, see notes.

Pour melted chocolate over bars and allow to cool (you can pop in the fridge to speed this up), then slice and serve.

NOTES: If you don't have a microwave, you can melt/blend topping together over the stovetop using the double boiler method: put vegan butter and chocolate chips in a small saucepan, and fill a larger saucepan with an inch or two of water. Place the small saucepan within the larger one (so it rests atop the water in the larger saucepan), and heat to a simmer, stirring until melted.

Acknowledgements

This book would not have been possible -quite literally- without the support of our beefless cake friends and family, who inspired this project and fueled it with their love and enthusiasm. Your generous spirits, in every facet of the gentle lives you lead, create a kinder world for all.

Alyssa Almond (p 98)
Karin (& Robert) Bills (p 75)
Michelle Carlson (p 69)
Kira Corbett (pp 60-61)
Stacy Crain (pp 120-121)
Kelly Denham (p 130)
Eric Dubs (p 72)
Dakota Gale (pp 12-13 + cover)
Jodi Grace (pp 3 + 141)
Felicia Greenfield (p 51)
Spencer Harber (p 54)
Kelsey Joseph (p 30)
Adar Kaltar (p 41)
Dylan Klein (p 80)

Derrick Lehman (p 110)
Sara Lehman (p 86)
Jeanne Leigh (p 137)
Annika Lundkvist (p 44)
Stefanie McGilp (p 84 + cover)
Kate (& Chris) Parente (p 71)
Ericka Rodriguez (p 95 + cover)
Michelle Russell (p 22)
Randy Schwartz (p 150)
David R. Smith (pp 38-39)
Taylor Wagner (pp 28-29)
Shawna Weaver (p 112)
Uncle Jesse the Vegan Wonder Doodle (p 146)

Special thanks also to Babs Schnedeker and Michelle Fetsch for their incredible contributions in proofreading and portrait photography.

Lastly, Robin would like to thank Jules for being the wind beneath her wings.

Jules would like to thank Robin for being the wind...well...this is awkward.

robin +
jules
proud founders of
PLANT-BASED *&* POINT

Share With Us

We love seeing your kitchen handiwork. Tag @plantbasedpoint across social media to share your creations!

"I am vegan for the animals and the environment. All the other health benefits are just an added bonus!"

Jodi Grace
Woodstock Farm Sanctuary

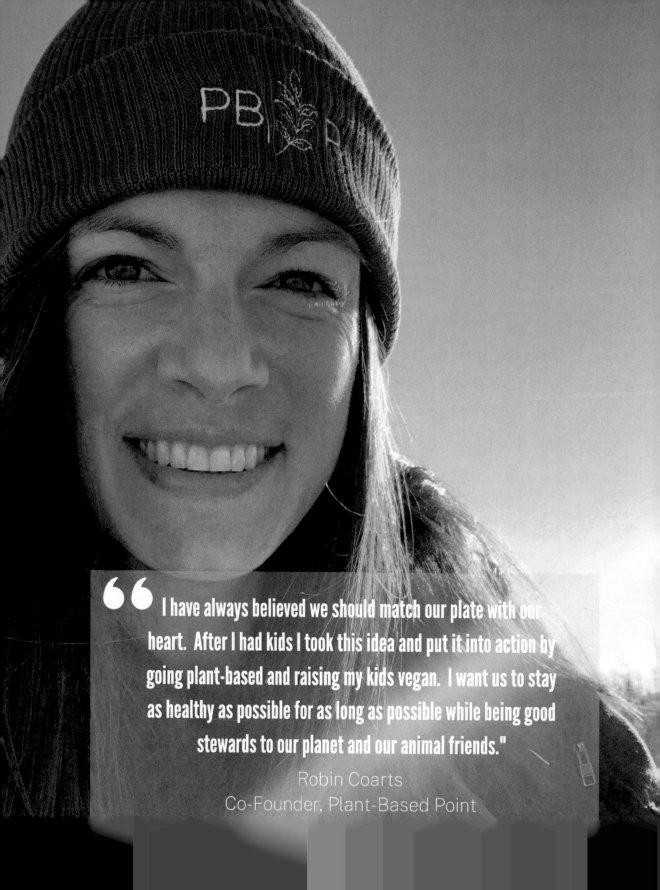

"I have always believed we should match our plate with our heart. After I had kids I took this idea and put it into action by going plant-based and raising my kids vegan. I want us to stay as healthy as possible for as long as possible while being good stewards to our planet and our animal friends."

Robin Coarts
Co-Founder, Plant-Based Point

About the Authors

ROBIN COARTS

After years of eating vegetarian, Robin made the leap to vegan shortly after having her first son. Fast forward a few years, and a few compelling books and documentaries later, and she and her whole family (husband and two sons) are enjoying plant-based eating and living. Along the way, Robin started doing presentations at local libraries on the benefits of eating plant-based. After meeting Jules and discovering a shared sense of humor and commitment to education, Plant-Based Point launched.

Robin holds an M.S. in thanatology, M.Ed in humane education, B.S in gerontology, B.S. in psychology, and a Plant-Based Nutrition Certificate from eCornell. When she's not busy cooking, learning about, or talking all things plant-based, you'll find her running after two sons, spending time with her husband, or hitting the trails.

> " I'm vegan because it's the simplest way to protect our health, non-human animals, and the single planet we share."
>
> Jules Schnedeker
> Co-Founder, Plant-Based Point

About the Authors

JULES SCHNEDEKER

Jules went vegan overnight in 2016 after watching the documentary, *Forks Over Knives*. She suddenly saw the impact our everyday food choices have on everything: the planet, non-human animals, and our health. In fact, this change was so transformative that Jules eventually quit her corporate job, moved across the country with nothing but her car and her dog, and put her money where her mouth was by co-founding Plant-Based Point.

Jules holds an M.A. in humane education, B.A. in creative writing, and a project management professional (PMP) certification. She's the author of the nonfiction humor blog, GoJulesGo.com, and when she's not busy telling her dog, Uncle Jesse, how cute he is, she's usually scouting new vegan products, trail running, or hiking the beautiful Oregon wilderness.

#1 beefless cake

INDEX

" Well into adulthood, I considered myself a meat eater. I thought I was keeping myself lean and healthy by focusing on protein in my diet, but things changed in my forties: My family expanded by two and I was diagnosed with an autoimmune disease. Luckily, one special lady opened my eyes to understanding that the diet I thought was healthy was actually detrimental to my health. At 43 I became vegan and said goodbye to my medications and health problems. I continue to be vegan for a better quality of life and to ensure I can keep up with my kids and be there for my family."

Randy Schwartz

Made in the USA
Las Vegas, NV
30 May 2021